ENERGY

Physical Science for Kids

ANDI DIEHN

Illustrated by Shululu

Nomad Press

A division of Nomad Communications

10 9 8 7 6 5

ISBN Softcover: 978-1-61930-641-7
ISBN Hardcover: 978-1-61930-639-4

Educational Consultant, Marla Conn

Questions regarding the ordering of this book should be addressed to
Nomad Press
2456 Christian St., White River Junction, VT 05001
www.nomadpress.net

Printed in the United States.

Other titles in this series:

  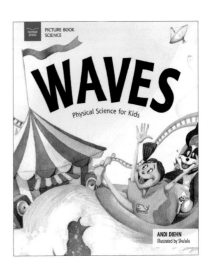

Check out more titles at www.nomadpress.net

Energy races through your feet,
Fueled with food and rest.

What happens when your
energy runs out?

Do you get cranky, tired,
and thrash about?

Have a snack! Take a snooze!

Keep your energy up and
you'll never lose!

Energy is everywhere, you
just need to look,

One thing for sure, you'll
find it in this book.

Has anyone ever told you, "You are full of energy?"

What are you doing when you're full of energy?
Maybe you are rolling on the ground and laughing.
Maybe you are running around the yard, leaping and
singing. Maybe you are sitting, but not sitting still.

What happens when your energy runs low?
People get sleepy, snoozy,
and slumpy when they
don't have enough energy.

FINISH

When you need energy,
you might reach
for a banana.

Or maybe some milk.
Or maybe a sandwich.

**You might even
fall sound asleep
on the floor!**

2%

4

Or maybe you'll take a break and lie in a hammock and look up at the sun peeking through the leaves on the trees.

And then . . .
your energy comes back!

Food and rest produce
energy in people.

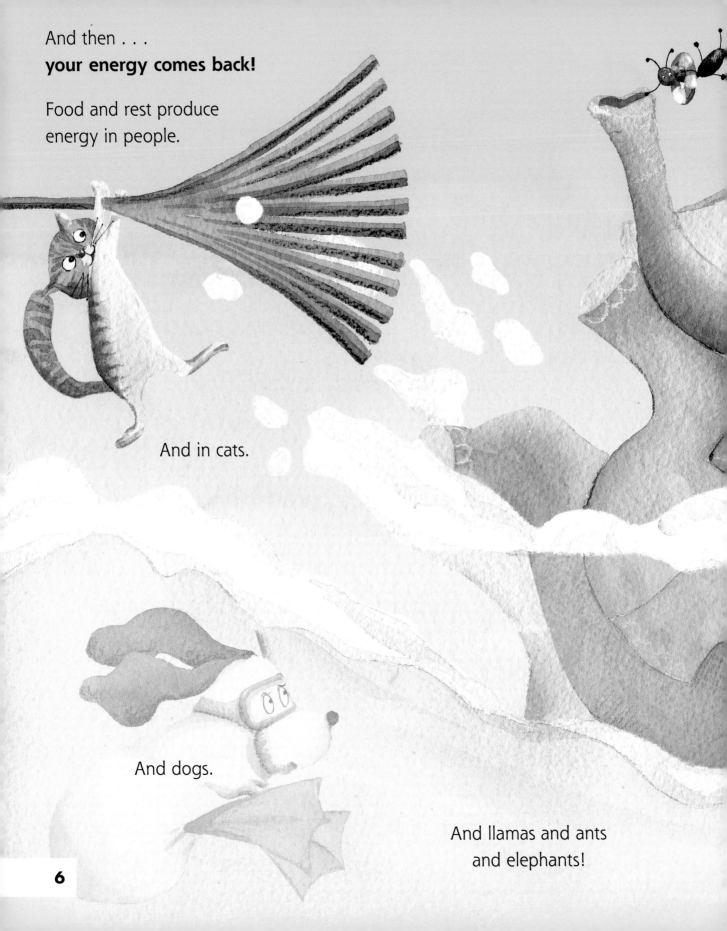

And in cats.

And dogs.

And llamas and ants
and elephants!

6

What else turns food
and rest into energy?

What about the plants in your kitchen window?

What about the weeds poking up through
the sidewalk? Trees and flowers and grass
don't run, leap, roll, and climb!

Do trees and plants and grass need energy?

Trees and flowers and grass DO need energy!
They need energy to grow. They need energy
to sprout new leaves. They need energy to
get strong enough to hold a hammock.

When a plant needs more
energy, it wilts.
It gets slumpy
(just like you do!).

Trees and flowers
and grass don't
eat bananas or
sandwiches or drink
milk. They don't
rest on the couch.
For some trees, that
would have to be
a really big couch!

12

Plants get energy by
drinking water and
absorbing sunlight.

Just like food and rest give you energy,
water and sunlight give energy to
trees and flowers and grass.

Energy from food is called chemical
energy, but not because you eat
stuff like cleaning chemicals for
breakfast, lunch, and dinner. **Yuck!**

Chemical energy is different from cleaning chemicals. When you eat bananas and sandwiches and drink milk, you are getting chemical energy from the food.

17

Other things use energy, too.
Look around your neighborhood.

**What do you
see that's
moving?**

Are there cars zooming past?
Are there airplanes in the sky?
Are there baseballs and basketballs
being tossed through the air?

Cars use energy to drive, airplanes use energy to fly, and balls need energy to zing from player to player.

Place a ball on the ground or floor. What does it do?

» Give the ball a push. Now what does it do?

» When did the ball have energy?

» When did it have no energy?

There are lots of different kinds of energy. Some energy comes from heat. Other energy comes from light. Plants use light energy to grow!

Energy from sunlight is called light energy.

Do you have a radio
inside your house?

That radio uses electrical energy!
So do lights, computers, and
your refrigerator. Energy makes
things work and move.

Energy is usually invisible. When you are running, can you see the energy coming off your body? **No!**

Can you see a tree using energy to grow taller and stronger? **No!**

Can you see energy inside your refrigerator, keeping your Jell-O cold? **No!**

We can't see
energy, but
we can feel it.

TRY THIS!

Rub your hands together.
Now rub them together faster!

» What happens?

» What do you feel?

**The heat that you
feel is heat energy.**

25

The only kind of energy we can see is light energy. Where do you see light energy?

You can see sunlight falling to earth.
You can see a beam coming from a flashlight.
You can see stars in the sky at night.

Energy is everywhere!

GLOSSARY

absorb: to soak up.

chemical energy: energy that comes from a chemical reaction. A chemical reaction can happen when two different chemicals mix together.

electrical energy: energy that is related to electricity.

energy: the power to work, grow, move, and do things.

heat energy: energy that comes from heat.

invisible: unable to be seen.

light energy: energy that comes from light.

sprout: to start growing.

wilt: to sag and start to fall down.

"The more of us musicians there are,
the crazier we all become."

— ERIK SATIE

Saint Cecilia, known as the special protector of all musicians